Jenny and the Jumble Sale

Written by
Sue Graves

Illustrated by
Richard Watson

W
FRANKLIN WATTS
LONDON • SYDNEY

Sue Graves

"Going to parties is always lots of fun. But I think the best parties of all are fancy dress parties, don't you?"

Richard Watson

"I hope you enjoy reading the book as much I enjoyed illustrating it!"

To

Jenny

Jenny was excited.

She was going to a party.

7

"It's a fancy dress party," Jenny
said. "But what shall I go as?"

9

"Let's go to the jumble sale," said Granny. "We'll get some good ideas there."

The jumble sale was very busy.

"Everyone look hard," said
Granny. "We need lots
of good ideas."

Hats

15

Tom found a toy helmet.

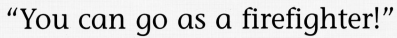

"You can go as a firefighter!"

he said.

Mum found some fairy wings.

18

"You can go as a fairy!" she said.

19

Dad found a silver suit.

20

"You can go as an astronaut!"
he said.

Grandad found some flippers
and a mask.

"You can go as a diver!" he said.

Granny found some clown's trousers. "You can go as a clown!" she said.

25

Jenny looked at all the things.
"But which shall I choose?"
she cried. "I like everything!"

27

"You must choose something!"
said Tom.

"I've got an idea," said Jenny.

"I shall go as ...

" ... a jumble sale!"

Notes for parents and teachers

READING CORNER has been structured to provide maximum support for new readers. The stories may be used by adults for sharing with young children. Primarily, however, the stories are designed for newly independent readers, whether they are reading these books in bed at night, or in the reading corner at school or in the library.

Starting to read alone can be a daunting prospect. **READING CORNER** helps by providing visual support and repeating words and phrases, while making reading enjoyable. These books will develop confidence in the new reader, and encourage a love of reading that will last a lifetime!

If you are reading this book with a child, here are a few tips:

1. Make reading fun! Choose a time to read when you and the child are relaxed and have time to share the story.

2. Encourage children to reread the story, and to retell the story in their own words, using the illustrations to remind them what has happened.

3. Give praise! Remember that small mistakes need not always be corrected.

READING CORNER covers three grades of early reading ability, with three levels at each grade. Each level has a certain number of words per story, indicated by the number of bars on the spine of the book, to allow you to choose the right book for a young reader:

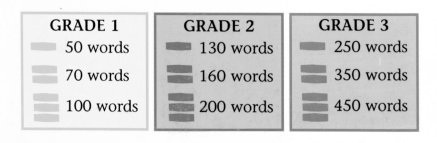

GRADE 1	GRADE 2	GRADE 3
50 words	130 words	250 words
70 words	160 words	350 words
100 words	200 words	450 words